The Colver Trading Method...For Winning The Commodity Game

The
Colver Trading Method
...For Winning The Commodity Game

By Jay C. Colver

WINDSOR BOOKS, BRIGHTWATERS, N.Y.

Published by Windsor Books
P. O. Box 280
Brightwaters, N.Y., 11718

CAVEAT: It should be noted that all commodity trades, patterns, charts, systems, etc., discussed in this book are for illustrative purposes only and are not to be construed as specific advisory recommendations. Further note that no method of trading or investing is foolproof or without difficulty, and past performance is no guarantee of future performance. All ideas and material presented are entirely those of the author and do not necessarily reflect those of the publisher or bookseller.

Finally! Speculating in commodity
futures becomes a game anyone
can win. The Colver System cuts through
all the myths, eliminates all the
guesswork and voodoo, and reveals probably the
simplest, most direct and most
profitable commodity futures trading
system yet published.

Contents

Introduction   **How and Why You and I Got Together** 9
                      Other Market Analysis Techniques Now Obsolete

Chapter One   **The Phenomenal Track Record**
                      Of The Colver System 13
                      What Can You Expect to Achieve?

Chapter Two   **The Myths & The Facts** 25
                      Success in this uncompromising business
                      requires that you abandon some old myths.

Chapter Three   **The Nuts & The Bolts** 33
                      Rub-A-Dub-Dub, Three Men in a Tub
                      You, The Speculator, Are The Missing Ingredient
                      How The Market Works For The Speculator
                      Margin
                      The Perfect "Computer"
                      So What Is This Fabulous Perfect "Computer?"
                      How To Profit If The Price Goes Down

Chapter Four   **The Four Laws Of Profit** 47
                      Four natural laws of economics which, if obeyed,
                      will assure your success.

Chapter Five   **The Ups And The Downs**
                      And How To Tell The Difference 55
                      How Much Money Does It Take To Start?
                      How To Keep Track Of The Ups And The Downs
                      The Key To My Trading System Is "The Signal"
                      How To Use "The Signal" To Buy And Sell
                      Using The Signal To Get Out
                      Never Meet A Margin Call

Chapter Six **The Complete Trading Plan** 65
Rule #1   Diversification
Rule #2   Consistency
Rule #3   Tithe Your Equity
Rule #4   Pyramid Your Profits
Choosing A Broker
You're On Your Way

Appendices

Appendix I   **Glossary** 75
Appendix II   **Bibliography** 77

Figures

1. 10
2. 15,16,17,18,19,20,21,22
2A 24
3. 35
4. 36,37
5. 41,42
6. 49
7. 50
8. 53
9. 58
10. 62
11. 64
12. 69

Introduction

The easiest and quickest way to get rich is to inherit a few million dollars. The second easiest and quickest way to such wealth could be speculating in the commodity futures market. Both of these avenues to wealth have their problems, of course, but the problems of inheriting wealth are pretty much insurmountable. In order to inherit millions you would have to be born to the right parents at the right time. And if that didn't happen to you, it is too late to do anything about it now. So assuming that you were not born to riches, that leaves speculating in commodity futures as probably the fastest, surest way to becoming financially independent.

Introduction

Of course, the main question when trading commodity futures is, which way is the price going to go next—up, down, or sideways. In recent years there have been some marvelous advances in the art of market analysis. Unfortunately, some of the best would drive even a mathematician crazy, let alone the average person like you and I. The traditional market analysis techniques are generally not more reliable or useful than blind, random selection. This little dart game has actually been proven to be more successful than some of them.

FIGURE #1

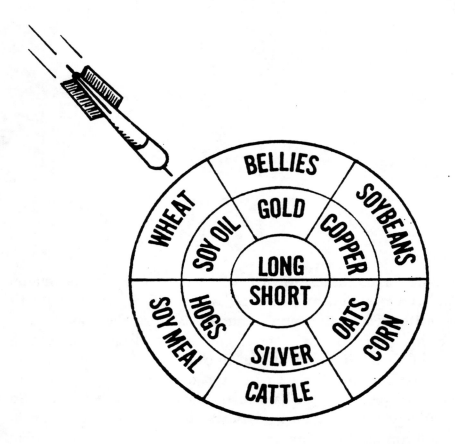

That's pretty discouraging to the speculator trying to figure out how to make his fortune in the market.

OTHER MARKET ANALYSIS
TECHNIQUES NOW OBSOLETE

Now there is a new way to trade commodity futures that makes all current market analysis techniques and price forecasting methods obsolete. I will show you how simple observation of the daily price charts will now tell you which way the market is heading each and every day. You won't be right every time, but 100% accuracy is not necessary to succeed. The market indicator or signal I have discovered gives a profitable trade from 40% to 50% of the time. This may not sound good enough, but the gains on average are three times larger than the losses. I will show you how to apply this new signal to the market, and I will also teach you to apply the four natural economic laws of profit to your trading in order to guarantee your success.

Chapter One

The Phenomenal Track Record
Of The Colver System

It has taken me fifteen years of winning and losing, trading and researching to finally develop this trading system. As I have traded commodities over the years, I was constantly searching for a consistent signal that would tell me which way prices were going to go. I knew there had to be a simple way. As I studied and tested all the various market analysis techniques available, I eventually cast them aside. It was clear to me that none of them were able to predict price movement with enough reliability to risk my money on.

Then one day I was studying the daily price charts and I noticed a pattern in the charts that seemed to happen each time the market changed direction. I researched this pattern over a number of years with all the major commodities. I found that it did correctly signal a change in the market direction 70% to 80% of the time. Then I integrated this signal into a total investment program which produced astounding profits.

WHAT CAN YOU EXPECT TO ACHIEVE?

What can you expect to achieve from my trading system? Of course, past performance does not guarantee similar performance in the future, and results will differ from one commodity to another, from one time period to another, from one broker to another, and from one investor to another, so the real future is up to you. Nevertheless, here are some representative results from the past, both distant and recent. The charts from 1981-1982 show that even in a major depression, the commodity futures market can be an astounding source of profit. As a matter of fact, the recovery period from a recession or depression is generally a very volatile and therefore profitable time for commodities.

These same results cannot be guaranteed for the future. However, the principles involved are fundamental to economics and human nature and are not likely to change. What I cannot control is how you and your broker will use these principles. It is my hope that you will find that they can lead you to financial freedom and independence.

This trading record may look formidable at first, but a little study will make it all clear.

The numbers in column one are for reference purposes when combined with the page number. They are used as in column 8. For example, the first trade was initiated on 7/29/81, as you can see on line one. The commodity was Copper (CP). The action taken was to buy copper long (L). The number of contracts was 16. The price was 92.2 and the margin required was $16,000.00. The margin deducted from the initial $162,000.00 in the account leaves a balance of $146,000.00 The trade was completed on line four. The date is 8/7/81. The reference number is 1-1, or page one line one. The action taken was to close out the position, all 16 contracts, at a price of 91.2 giving you a loss of 1¢/lb. One cent in copper is worth $250.00 so your

FIGURE #2

Page 1   ACCOUNT ALL 10 COMMODITIES   STARTING BALANCE: $162,000

No.	Date	Commodity	Action	Contr.	Price	Margin	Ref No.	Action	Contr.	Price	Comis'n	Net	Distr.	Balance
1	7/29/81	CP	L	16	92.2	16,000								146,000
2	7/30	BO	S	11	25.6	14,300								131,700
3	8/6	G	L	4	450	12,000								119,700
4	8/7	CP			91.2		1-1	Out	16	91.2	1048	(5048)		130,652
5	8/7	CP	S	13	91.2	13,000								117,652
6	8/11	CP			93.5		1-5	Out	13	93.5	951.5	8246.5		122,325.5
7	8/11	CP	L	12	93.5	12,000								110,325.5
8	8/18	CP			93.4		1-7	Out	12	93.4	786	(1086)		121,239.5
9	8/18	CP	S	12	93.4	12,000								109,239.5
10	8/24	SB	S	5	745	11,000								98,239.5
11	8/27	LC	L	9	65.1	9,900								88,339.5
12	9/2	CP			87.7		1-9	Out	12	87.7	786	16314		116,653.5
13	9/2	BO			23.45		1-2	Out	11	23.95	676.5	10213.5		141,167
14	9/3	CP	L	14	88.4	14,000								127,167
15	9/3	BO	L	10	24.45	13,000								114,167
16	9/3	SI	L	6	1107	12,000								124,167
17	9/4	PB	L	5	69	10,000								92,167
18	9/6	CP			84.3		1-14	Out	14	84.3	917	(5267)		90,900
19	9/8	BO			23.8		1-15	Out	10	23.8	615	4515		99,385
20	9/8	G			487		1-3	Out	4	487	400	14440		125,785
21	9/8	C	S	14	326	12,600								113,185
22	9/10	SM	L	7	216.6	11,200								101,985
23	9/11	PB			70.8		1-17	Out	5	70.8	325	3095		115,080
24	9/15	CP	L	12	87.6	12,600								103,080
25	9/15	S3			765		1-10	Out	5	765	350	(5350)		108,730
26	9/16	SI			1240		1-16	Out	6	1240	309	79491		200,221
27	9/17	CP			84.1		1-24	Out	12	84.1	786	(11286)		200,935
28	9/17	G	S	7	492	21,000								179,935
29	9/17	SI	S	9	1191	18,000								161,135

15

FIGURE #2 CONT'D

Page 2   ACCOUNT ALL 10

No	Date	Commodity	Action	Contr.	Price	Margin	Ref No	Action	Contr.	Price	Comisn	Net	Distr	Balance
1	9/18	SM					1-22	OUT	7	2167	4305	(360.5)		172,774.5
2	9/21	G					1-28	OUT	7	520	700	(2980)		173,474.5
3	9/21	G	L	6	520	18,000								155,474.5
4	9/23	PB	S	8	65.65	16,000								139,474.5
5	9/23	LH	S	13	48	14,700								125,174.5
6	9/25	BO	S	10	22.65	13,000								112,174.5
7	9/27	SI					1-29	OUT	9	1020	463.5	15348.5		283,611
8	9/29	PB					2-4	OUT	8	65.85	520	(128)		298,483
9	9/29	SI	L	15	1025	30,000								268,483
10	9/30	C					1-21	OUT	14	318.5	910	4340		185,413
11	9/30	C	L	32	318.5	28,800								256,613
12	10/2	BO					2-6	OUT	10	22.95	615	(2415)		247,208
13	10/5	RO	L	21	23.48	27,300								239,908
14	10/7	BO					2-13	OUT	21	23.65	1291.5	850.5		218,056.5
15	10/12	G					2-3	OUT	6	487	600	(9200)		94,858.5
16	10/12	SI					2-9	OUT	15	1027	772.5	2227.5		229,086
17	10/13	CP	S	30	82.2	30,000								263,086
18	10/16	BO	S	21	23.1	27,300								244,786
19	10/16	G	S	8	482	24,000								217,786
20	10/16	SB	S	20	739	22,000								195,786
21	10/17	LC					1-11	OUT	9	65.5	630	810		206,476
22	10/19	SI	S	10	1008	20,000								186,496
23	10/19	LH					2-5	OUT	13	47.15	845	2470		203,266
24	10/20	C					2-11	OUT	32	319	2080	(2880)		229,186
25	10/22	G					2-19	OUT	8	473	800	6400		259,586
26	10/22	SI					2-22	OUT	10	1006	515	1485		281,071
27	10/23	SI	L	14	1015	28,000								253,071
28	10/30	BO					2-18	OUT	21	23	1291.5	31.5		280,339.5
29	10/30	SI					2-27	OUT	14	1009	721	9121		279,218.5

16

FIGURE #2 CONT'D

Page 3   ACCOUNT ALL 10

No	Date	Commodity	Action	Contr.	Price	Margin	Ref No	Action	Contr.	Price	Comis'n	Net	Distr.	Balance
1	10/30	PB	S	15	68.9	30,000								269,218.5
2	11/2	BO	L	21	23.2	27,300								241,918.5
3	11/2	SI	S	12	1000	24,000								217,918.5
4	11/3	LC	S	20	64	22,000								195,918.5
5	11/4	BO					3-2	OUT	21	22.8	1291.5	(6331.5)		216,887
6	11/4	PB					3-1	OUT	15	69.5	975	(4395)		242,492
7	11/4	PB	L	12	69.5	24,000								218,492
8	11/4	LH	L	20	47.6	22,000								196,492
9	11/5	C	S	22	316.5	19,800								176,692
10	11/5	LC					3-4	OUT	20	64.9	1400	(8600)		190,092
11	11/5	BO	S	15	22.72	19,500								110,592
12	11/10	SM	S	11	205.6	17,600								152,792
13	11/10	G	S	5	442	15,000								137,992
14	11/11	PB					3-7	OUT	12	68.9	780	(3516)		158,476
15	11/12	LH					3-8	OUT	20	47.3	1300	3100		177,376
16	11/12	CP					2-17	OUT	30	77.3	1965	9,785		227,161
17	11/12	PB	S	11	68.4	22,000								205,161
18	11/12	LH	S	19	47.3	20,900								184,261
19	11/16	CP	S	18	77.1	18,000								166,261
20	11/17	C	+S	20	305	18,000								148,261
21	11/18	LC	S	13	63.4	14,300								133,961
22	11/20	SM					3-12	OUT	11	201	616.5	4383.5		155,944.5
23	11/24	C	+S	21	294	18,900								137,044.5
24	11/25	G	L	5	434	15,000								140,544.5
25	11/25	G					3-13	OUT	5	434	500	3500		125,544.5
26	11/27	SI					3-3	OUT	12	873	618	127,782		277,326.5
27	11/30	SM	L	17	201	27,200								252,126.5
28	12/1	SB					2-20	OUT	20	700	1400	37,600		309,726.5
29	12/2	CP					2-19	OUT	18	80.1	1179	(15,129)		312,597.5

17

FIGURE #2 CONT'D

Page 4   ACCOUNT ALL 10

No	Date	Commodity	Action	Contr.	Price	Margin	Ref No.	Action	Contr.	Price	Comis'n	Net	Distr.	Balance
1	12/2	CP	L	31	80.1	31,000								281,597.5
2	12/3	LC	+S	27	61.4	29,700								251,897.5
3	12/3	SI	L	13	922	26,000								225,897.5
4	12/7	SM	—	—	—	—	3-27	OUT	17	200.6	1045.5	(1735.5)		251,572
5	12/7	G	—	—	—	—	3-25	OUT	5	440	500	2500		268,872
6	12/7	C	+S	36	288	32,400								236,472
7	12/7	LH	+S	95	41	27,500								208,972
8	12/8	G	S	7	432	21,000								181,972
9	12/8	SM	S	12	193	19,920								168,772
10	12/8	CP	—	—	—	—	4-1	OUT	31	77.7	200.5	(20,630.5)		179,141.5
11	12/9	SI	—	—	—	—	4-3	OUT	13	918	669.5	(5869.5)		179,272
12	12/9	CP	S	20	75.9	20,000								179,272
13	12/10	SI	S	9	900	18,000								161,272
14	12/10	SI	—	—	—	—	4-13	OUT	9	943	463.5	39,163.5		140,108.5
15	12/10	CP	—	—	—	—	4-12	OUT	20	77.5	1310	9310		150,798.5
16	12/10	G	—	—	—	—	4-8	OUT	7	446	700	10,500		161,298.5
17	12/17	CP	L	16	77.9	16,000								145,298.5
18	12/17	LH	—	—	—	—	4-7 / 3-18	OUT	44	38.75	2860	62,750		256,448.5
19	12/17	LC	—	—	—	—	4-2 / 3-21	OUT	40	56.6	2800	105,200		405,648.5
20	12/17	P3	—	—	—	—	3-17	OUT	11	56.95	715	47,146		454,074
21	12/17	PB	L	22	56.95	44,000								390,094.5
22	12/18	LC	L	35	56.75	38,500								351,594.5
23	12/21	G	S	12	422	36,000								315,594.5
24	12/21	SI	S	16	881	32,000								283,594.5
25	12/22	LC	—	—	—	—	4-22	OUT	35	54.8	2450	(29,750)		292,344.5
26	12/24	SM	—	—	—	—	4-9	OUT	12	191.5	738	1062		312,606.5
27	12/24	C	—	—	—	—	3-29 / 4-6	OUT	99	278.5	6435	152,740		476,916.5
28	12/24	BO	—	—	—	—	3-11	OUT	15	20.3	922.5	208,575		537,304
29	12/24	BO	L	41	20.3	53,300								484,004

18

FIGURE #2 CONT'D

ACCOUNT __ALL 10__

No.	Date	Commodity	Action	Contr.	Price	Margin	Ref No.	Action	Contr.	Price	Com'ish	Net	Distr.	Balance
1	12/24	SM	L	30	191.5	48,000								436,004
2	12/24	C	L	48	478.5	43,200								392,804
3	12/28	LH	L	36	43.3	39,600								353,204
4	12/29	LC	S	32	54.65	35,200								318,004
5	12/30	G					4-23	OUT	12	403	1200	2,600		375,604
6	12/30	SI					4-24	OUT	16	878	824	3976		411,580
7	12/30	BO					4-29	OUT	41	20	2521.5	9901.5		454,978.5
8	12/31	BO	S	35	19.8	45,500								409,478.5
9	1/6	LC					5-4	OUT	32	56.9	2240	3,040		413,638.5
10	1/6	CP					4-17	OUT	16	75.9	1048	9,048		420,590.5
11	1/6	SB	L	19	664	41,800								378,790.5
12	1/7	BO					5-8	OUT	35	20.24	2152.5	11,392.5		412,848
13	1/8	SB					5-11	OUT	19	660	1330	5,130		449,568
14	1/8	LC	L	41	57.9	45,100								404,468
15	1/11	SB	S	18	656	39,600								364,868
16	1/4	G	S	12	403	36,000								328,868
17	1/11	SM					5-1	OUT	30	192.4	1845	855		377,723
18	1/13	SB					5-15	OUT	18	662	1260	660		410,663
19	1/14	SB	L	19	669	41,800								318,863
20	1/14	BO	L	28	2004	36,400								332,463
21	1/14	SM	L	21	196	33,600								298,463
22	1/21	CP	S	30	74.2	30,000								248,863
23	1/22	SM					5-21	OUT	21	195.5	1291.5	(2341.5)		300,121.5
24	1/25	SM	S	19	193.9	30,400								169,721.5
25	1/25	LC					5-14	OUT	41	60.1	2870	33,210		348,031.5
26	1/25	LC	S	32	60.1	35,200								312,831.5
27	1/26	CP					5-22	OUT	30	74.9	1965	5715		349,716.5
28	1/26	CP	L	34	74.9	34,000								306,716.5
29	1/27	SM					5-24	OUT	19	199.1	1168.5	11,048.5		326,068

FIGURE #2 CONT'D

Page 6   ACCOUNT ALLIO

No	Date	Comodity	Action	Contr.	Price	Margin	Ref No.	Action	Contr.	Price	Comis'n	Net	Distr.	Balance
1	1/27	S1	L	16	861	32,000								294,068
2	1/29	LC					5-26	OUT	32	61.7	2240	22,720		306,588
3	1/29	LC	L	28	61.7	30,800								275,748
4	2/4	G					5-16	OUT	12	403	120	(120)		310,548
5	2/4	SB					5-19	OUT	19	680	1330	9120		361,468
6	2/4	BO					5-20	OUT	28	20.55	492	8076		405,944
7	2/4	SB	S	18	680	33,600								366,944
8	2/4	G	L	12	403	36,000								383,344
9	2/5	PB					4-21	OUT	22	72.6	1430	129,404		503,748
10	2/5	SM	S	31	195.8	49,600								454,148
11	2/6	PB	S	23	70.6	46,000								405,148
12	2/8	C					5-9	OUT	48	282.5	3120	6460		457,828
13	2/8	LH					5-3	OUT	36	47.65	2340	44,640		542,068
14	2/8	LH	S	49	47.65	53,900								488,168
15	2/8	C	S	54	282.5	48,600								439,568
16	2/8	BO	S	34	20.02	44,200								395,568
17	2/9	CP					5-28	OUT	34	73.7	962	10,462		418,906
18	2/12	S1					6-1	OUT	16	912	824	29,776		531,682
19	2/16	S1	S	27	900	54,000								477,682
20	2/19	C	+S	57	275	51,500								426,382
21	2/19	PB					6-11	OUT	31	705	2015	(3193)		469,189
22	2/19	G					6-8	OUT	12	378	1200	(3120)		473,989
23	2/20	G	S	16	377	48,000								425,989
24	2/22	PB	L	21	72.4	42,000								383,989
25	2/23	LH					6-14	OUT	49	48.55	3165	16,415		421,074
26	2/23	CP	S	42	72.1	42,000								379,474
27	2/24	G					6-23	OUT	16	380	1600	6400		421,074
28	2/25	PB					6-24	OUT	21	72.3	1365	2163		460,911
29	2/26	SM					6-10	OUT	31	189.9	1906.5	16,283.5		526,894.5

ACCOUNT **ALL 10**

No.	Date	Commodity	Action	Contr.	Price	Margin	Ref No.	Action	Contr.	Price	Comisn	Net	Distr.	Balance
1	2/26	SB					6-7	OUT	18	649	1260	26,640		593,134.5
2	2/26	LC					6-3	OUT	28	64.25	1960	26,600		650,534.5
3	2/26	LC	S	59	64.25	64,900								585,634.5
4	2/26	PB	S	99	70.2	58,000								527,634.5
5	2/26	LH	S	48	45.8	52,800								474,834.5
6	2/26	G	S	16	372	48,000								426,834.5
7	3/1	SM	L	27	190.1	43,200								383,634.5
8	3/2	LC					7-3	OUT	59	65.3	4130	28,910		419,624.5
9	3/2	LH					7-5	OUT	48	47.45	3120	26,880		445,544.5
10	3/3	PB					7-4	OUT	29	72.4	1885	26,129		477,415.5
11	3/3	C					6-15 / 6-20	OUT	111	273	7215	24,142.5		601,458
12	3/3	C	L	67	273	60,300								541,158
13	3/4	SM					7-7	OUT	27	186.6	1660.5	11,110.5		573,247.5
14	3/8	C					7-12	OUT	67	268.5	4355	19,430		614,117.5
15	3/8	C	S	68	268.5	61,200								552,917.5
16	3/9	G					7-6	OUT	16	343	1600	44,800		645,117.5
17	3/9	LH	L	59	49.9	64,900								580,817.5
18	3/9	PB	L	29	75.4	58,000								522,817.5
19	3/10	CP					6-26	OUT	42	69.4	2751	95,599		520,416.5
20	3/10	BO					6-16	OUT	34	18.61	2091	26,673		661,289.5
21	3/10	SI					6-19	OUT	27	758	1390.5	382,002	1,087,299	1,087,299
22	3/10	G	L	37	347	111,000								986,299
23	3/11	SM	L	62	185	68,200								918,099
24	3/12	G					7-22	OUT	37	327	3700	77,700		951,399
25	3/12	G	S	32	327	96,000								855,399
26	3/12	LC	L	78	67.25	85,800								769,599
27	3/15	PB					7-18	OUT	29	72.9	1885	29,435		748,164
28	3/16	PB	S	40	71.5	80,000								781,164
29	3/18	PB					7-28	OUT	40	74.6	2600	47,120		887,564

21

FIGURE #2 CONT'D

Page 8   ACCOUNT ALL 10

NO	Date	Commodity	Action	Contr.	Price	Margin	Ref No	Action	Contr.	Price	Comisn	Net	Distr.	Balance
1	3/18	G					7-25	OUT	32	332	3200	(19,200)		864,484
2	3/19	LH					7-17	OUT	59	50.05	3835	152,810		1,012,194
3	3/22	G	L	36	332	108,000								974,194
4	3/22	SB	L	44	646	96,800								877,394
5	3/25	SI	S	44	735	88,000								789,394
6	4/2	SI					8-5	OUT	44	741	2200	(28,600)		848,728
7	4/2	LC					7-26	OUT	78	69.3	5460	58,500		793,020
8	4/2	G					6-3	OUT	36	337	3600	14,400		1,115,428
9	4/2	SM					7-23	OUT	62	192	3813	39,587		1,223,215
10	4/2	C					7-15	OUT	68	276	4420	(29,920)		1,354,445
11	4/3	SB					8-4	OUT	44	659	3080	25,520		1,316,815
12														
13														
14							GAIN: $1,214,815							
15							% GAIN: 750%							
16							TIME: 249 days							
17							ANNUALIZED GAIN: $1,780,753							
18							ANNUALIZED % GAIN: 999%							
19														
20							Total Trades: 104	%				Total $		Ave. Trade *
21							Profitable Trades: 48	46%				$920,518.50		$42,490.43
22							Losing Trades: 56	54%				$794,865.50		$14,195.03
23														
24							*Average gain is almost 3 times the average loss (2.972)							

22

transaction looks like this: 92.2 − 91.2 = 1, 1 x 16 x $250 = $4,000. The commission was $65.50/contract or $1,048.00 total, which should be added to the $4,000.00 giving the net loss of $5,048.00.

Your account balance was $119,700.00. With the $5,048.00 and the return of your $16,000.00 margin, the new balance is $130,652.00.

The same day, after getting out of copper, because your signal said to go short, you took the position recorded on line five. Copper (CP) short 13 contracts. You can only short 13 contracts because the margin is $1,000.00 and your balance is $130,652.00. Later in the book you will see that I recommend that you only use 10% of your assets when taking a position in the market. Your new balance is $117,652.00.

This pattern is followed throughout the trading record.

Fig. 2A[1] shows graphically how your account grew during this nine month period. The dashed line smooths the curve and clearly shows that the growth of this type of account is logarithmic. Basically, this reflects the enormous profit potential inherent in a carefully managed pyramiding program.

1. Fig. 2A: These results are typical of the results using the Colver Method. Similar results have been possible throughout at least the last 10 years. I can't guarantee the future—but the past certainly has shown me some excellent results!

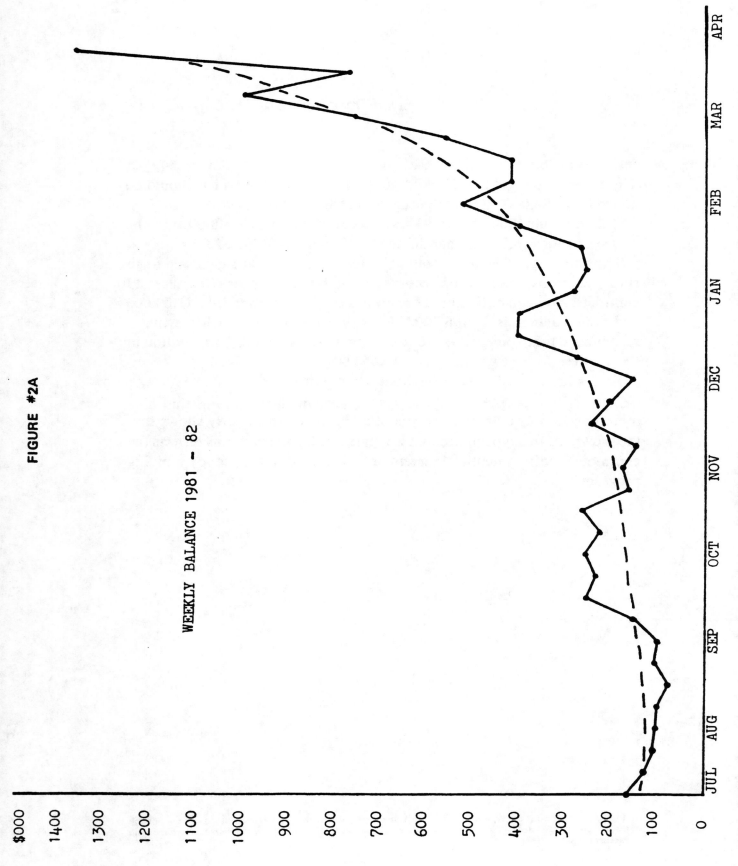

FIGURE #2A

WEEKLY BALANCE 1981 – 82

24

Chapter Two

The Myths & The Facts

Whoever said, "There ain't no free lunch." had terrible grammar, but an excellent grasp of reality. I'm sure you know from your own experience that everything in life has its price. Most of the time, however, the price we pay for the things we want is composed of a little of both time and money. As a simple case in point, let's consider what you're doing right now. You have given up some of your hard earned money for this book, and, in addition, you are now giving up some of your precious time to read it. In return for this investment of your time and money, you rightfully expect this book to deliver on its promise to help you make money. This book promises to teach you how to become a successful speculator in the commodity futures market. So right here I want to dispel seven myths about this business.

Myth #1: Learning Some Technique Will Make Me Successful.
Fact: Learning A Technique Alone Cannot Make You Successful.

In this book I will show you how to do things which, if applied correctly in the actual market, will make you a successful commodity speculator. It is not difficult, but you must study, you must apply the things you learn here. You must trade the market and you must transform yourself into a successful speculator. I have no intention of apologizing for such an obvious fact. I do it to clear my conscience. If you're a dreamer rather than a doer, I don't suppose there is anything I can say to change you. We all dream from time to time. But if you just read this book and dream about the money you could make but never go into the real market and apply the technique, you cannot say that I didn't warn you. However, this time, please don't dream about it. *Go Do It!*

Myth #2: Some People Get All The Breaks.
Fact: We Make Our Own Breaks.

Everyone does something to make a living. Even going to the unemployment office is doing something. But different work pays off differently. Some work pays one to one, some work pays ten to one, and some work pays a thousand to one. For example, let's say that you want to be a builder. You could set to work with your own hands and build your own home. When you were finished you would have one house, for possibly six months invested time. Or you might try another approach. You could become a contractor, and for six months of labor performed by yourself, your employees, and your subcontractors, you could build ten houses. Then, on the other hand, you might become an architect, and from six months labor at the drawing board, comes a tract of one thousand homes, plus churches, schools, a park and a recreation center. In each case, the same amount of time and effort on your part produced vastly different results.

I'm not judging the validity of any of these approaches. You are free to choose what you want to do with your life, and if you are happy and ful-filled, who am I or anyone else to say that you have chosen the wrong approach? However, remember this: if you are not happy and are not fulfilled, the hard truth is that you have no one to blame but yourself. You have chosen the outcome because you have chosen the road to travel and the means of getting there.

Am I saying that you are totally to blame for your present condition and degree of success? Yes, I am. But please spare me the brickbats. I can hear your cry of outrage and wounded pride from here. I hear you saying that you are not to blame. That your lack of success and your unhappy life are the result of bad luck, a bad marriage, your business partner, your broker, your mother-in-law, the Russians, the CIA, the weather,_____(fill in the blank). Certainly not you, right? Well, if you are convinced that someone else, or some circumstance, or fate or whatever, is responsible for your present plight, far be it from me to try to convince you otherwise. However, if you want to become successful, I suggest that you assume the attitude of total responsibility for your life. If you will just *act as if* you, and you alone, are totally responsible for where you go from here, it will be enough to transform you into the successful person that you think you want to be, and that I believe you ought to be.

How would you characterize what you are now doing to make a living? Does it pay you 1 to 1, does it pay you 10 to 1, or does it pay you 1000 to 1? Speculating in commodity futures can pay 1000 to 1 or more, if you learn to do it correctly. That is what this book is all about.

Myth #3: There are Experts Who Know Better Than I How To Manage My Money.
Fact: No One Can Manage Your Money Better Than You.

We have all grown accustomed to relying upon experts. We call in the experts for everything from fixing the plumbing to raising our children. In the area of your financial independence, you must become the expert. It is too important to leave to someone else, no matter how skilled and experienced. No matter how well intentioned, or what they may say, if you go to someone else to manage your financial affairs, their primary objective will be *their* financial well-being. They cannot help it, their income is the thing which is uppermost in their minds. You will always come second. Brokers, of course, are the worst. It is very unlikely that they will be expert traders, since they are primarily salesmen. They make their commission whenever you trade the market, regardless of whether you make money or lose money. Of course, they want you to make money because if you do, you will continue to trade and create commissions for them. But their primary interest is putting bread on their tables and gas in their Rolls Royce's, and there are plenty of new clients where you came from.

Myth #4: Making A Fortune Will Make Me Happy.
Fact: One Man's Success Is Another Man's Ho Hum.

What is the meaning of success? Success means different things to different people. To me, it means that at the end of each month there is a big plus on the bottom line of my financial statement. I can't believe how many people lose sight of this fundamental objective. If your objective is net profits, everything else will fall into place. With financial success and achievement all the other objectives can be met. This is especially true when you realize how little of your precious time will be required to achieve financial success by trading commodity futures. Generally, a person who has made a lot of money on his own has not had the time for the other important things in life. You will have plenty of time. In fact, it will be very difficult for you to spend more than an hour a day studying and trading the market when you use my system.

If your objective is the glamour and excitement of trading, that's okay, but just remember that with glamour and excitement as your goal, sooner or later you will lose all your money. When your money is gone, you can no longer enjoy the glamour and excitement of trading. So your objective still should be net profits.

If ego motivates you, if you want to be known as an expert, if you want to be recognized as an authority in your field, you can, if you are successful. But you will only be successful if you continue to make money. So, again, net profits should be your primary objective.

If it's the contest that motivates you, I hope you'll remember that the real contest is not between you and the market. The market is totally impersonal and is definitely not at war with you. The contest is not between you and the other traders. You do not make more money if they make less, or less if they make more. For all practical purposes, they do not know that you exist. If there is a contest, and there is, it is between you and yourself. If you want to win the contest, you must overcome your own problems. Your main problem is fear, and fear comes from ignorance. When you have learned how to apply the principles and procedures outlined here, you will have overcome ignorance. You will know what to do under any and all circumstances, and that knowledge will give you confidence. The truth is that if you follow the instructions given here, your speculating will be a simple and pleasant journey as you flow along in harmony with the laws of nature towards greater and greater financial independence. How much money you make will be entirely up to you.

Myth #5: Commodity Speculation Is Only For Gamblers And Is Somehow Immoral.
Fact: Commodity Speculation Is One Of The Last Bastions Of True Free Enterprise.

Commodity speculation is free enterprise in its most elementary form. This quote from Noah Webster best describes what speculation is, "...to take a risk in order to gain some advantage." This definition applies to every business and, like every other business in the world, the commodity speculator tries to keep his risk at a minimum and his profits at a maximum. He tries to buy low and sell high, and to keep his costs and expenses below his income. However, let's say that you own your own business—a clothing store, for example. You buy four times a year for the seasons. You have basically four chances in a year to make a profit, because, if you don't buy right, there is no way you can sell right. And even then, if fashions or economic conditions should change unexpectedly, you may have to mark some of your merchandise down to below cost in order to move it out.

When you're trading commodity futures, you could have four chances a week, or even four chances a day, to make a profit. You'll do more buying and selling, more profiting and losing, in a month than most businessmen will do in a year or more.

Commodity speculation is free enterprise, boiled down and condensed to the bare essentials: 1. evaluating risk, 2. investing your money, 3. winning or losing. You sell but never deliver, you buy but never take delivery. You provide an essential service, but you never meet any of the people you serve.

Because it is so pure and elementary, with so many opportunities to make or lose money every day, most people are not suited for this form of business. It is a very fast-paced business and when you are in the market, you must be on the job every day. You don't invest in commodities like you do in stocks. You trade commodity futures and many times you will be in and out of a trade overnight. You must be self-confident, decisive and willing to live with the results of your decisions. On the positive side, you are in complete control of your life. You are not dependent upon the whims of customers, clients or bosses. It is just you and the market. When you want to take a day off, or a vacation, just close out all your positions and relax. The market will always be there waiting for you when you come back.

Myth #6: It Takes A Lot Of Research.
Fact: It Takes No Research At All!

The truly revolutionary thing about what I have discovered is that once you learn my Market Direction Signals, you will know by simple observation which direction the market will go each and every day. From now on you will be the one with the inside information. From now on *you will be the expert!* Do not listen to brokers. Do not listen to analysts. Do not subscribe to advisory services. Do not even subscribe to a chart service. Absolutely the only expense you will have will be a little chart paper, pencils, and brokerage commissions.

Myth #7: Avoid All Get-Rich-Quick Schemes.
Fact: Today, The Only Way To Get Rich *Is* Quick.

As we go along through life, our definitions of words sometimes drift off course until the words we use come to mean something quite different than what they were intended to mean. In such a dilemma, a good dictionary acts as a sure rudder to keep our thinking on course. According to Webster, a scheme is "a carefully arranged and systematic program of action for attaining some object." I think that is a very accurate description of what I am offering you. And as for the word "quick," the truth is, that it is virtually impossible to get rich slow today. There have been some people in the past who have saved their money and eventually gotten rich, but that was before the days of inflation as we know it today. If you put your money into any savings plan, inflation and taxes will erode it faster than any available amount of interest will cause it to grow. Therefore, if you save your money today, you will get poorer every day. That's right, *saving is the road to the poorhouse.*

That being the case, any method, scheme or system designed to help you get rich today must be designed to help you get rich quickly. At least it will have to be quick by pre-inflation standards. Quick is also a relative term. To some people it might mean overnight. Overnight riches come only to sweepstakes and lottery winners, or jackpot winners in Las Vegas, and inheritors of someone else's wealth. These avenues are almost entirely dependent upon luck. And luck cannot be calculated into a plan to make money because it cannot be controlled. If there is any such thing as luck, it might better be described as an opportunity which comes to a person who is prepared to take advantage of it, and who is in the right place at the right time. Many such opportunities will come to you in the commodity market, and you will be prepared to take advantage of them. This program does not, however, rely upon luck. Maybe you think a year would be quick. A year is very reasonable, depending on what you mean by rich. Let me summarize it this way.

**If You Will Do As I Tell You, You Should Be
Completely Independent of Other Sources of Income
Within One Year. And That's a Fact!**

Chapter Three

The Nuts And The Bolts

I approach this chapter with some misgivings because, even though I believe that you should know as much as possible about the business you are getting into, sometimes too much knowledge can be a dangerous thing. One of the best examples of this problem occurred in 1973. That was the year the Russians first bought so much wheat from us. At that time, quite a few very knowledgeable traders lost a bundle trading the market, especially in soybeans. The reason they lost, instead of making huge profits, as they should have, was that they knew too much. These men were real experts. They knew more about soybeans than the farmers who grew them. Consequently, when the unexpected happened, they couldn't deal with it.

The Nuts and The Bolts

Figure #3 shows how the price of soybeans reacted to the Russian wheat purchase. The price of most commodities went up sharply, but the increase in the price of soybeans was the most spectacular. Most traders made a lot of money until about point A. Then, because they were experts and they *knew* that the price of soybeans had never been higher, and should not go higher than $4.00 a bushel, they began to sell soybeans short. They *knew* that the price was about to go down. Well, you can see what it did. It did begin to fall, in apparent confirmation of their wisdom, or because of their expectations, but then the true market forces took over again, and the price rose to almost $5.00 a bushel (point B.). Now anyone who hadn't gotten out at $4.00 got out and got short, *knowing* that the price *had* to fall this time. But again, the market said, "buy, buy" and went all the way to $8.50 (point C.), which was obviously the right price for soybeans at that time, because that is where it leveled out. Those expert traders who knew how to trade soybeans were trapped in their short positions and lost their shirts.

Incidently, my system would have traded soybeans as indicated in Fig. #4, for a profit of $224,050.00, which was a return on investment of 1,020%.

This is just one of the more dramatic stories that illustrate the unusual fact that knowing a lot about a particular commodity can sometimes be disastrous. Many smaller disasters occur every day, with investors leaving the market broke because they thought they were smarter than the market.

Always maintain a healthy respect for the market. The commodity market is like the ocean; huge and powerful and very treacherous to the unwary. And, just as many have on the ocean, many have made huge fortunes on the commodity market, but no one has ever conquered it. With that note of caution, we'll proceed to examine the workings of this market so that you can make your fortune out of it.

RUB-A-DUB-DUB, THREE MEN IN A TUB

This huge and treacherous ocean, called the commodity futures market, is used principally by three groups of people: producers, processors and speculators.

Producers grow, mine or otherwise create the commodities for sale to the processors and consumers.

FIGURE #3

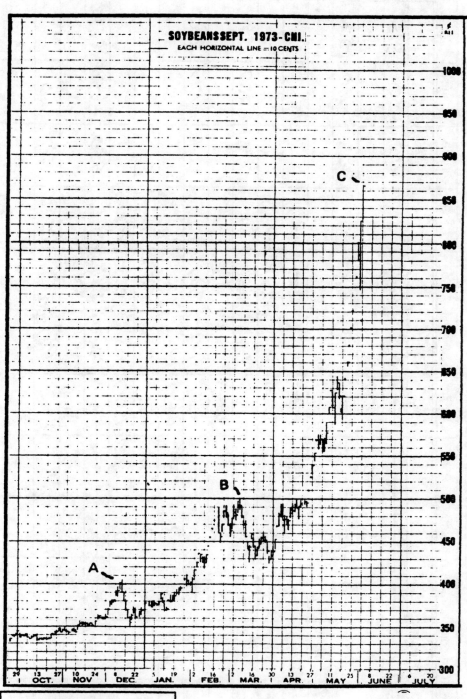

SOYBEANS SEPT. 1973 - CHI.
EACH HORIZONTAL LINE = 10 CENTS

35

FIGURE #4

Page _____ ACCOUNT 1972-73 Soybeans

No.	Date	Commodity	Action	Contr.	Price	Margin	Ref No.	Action	Contr.	Price	Comis'n	Net	Distr.	Balance
														20,000
1	10/25	Soybeans	L	1	351	1500								18,500
2	12/5	"	S	2	407	3000	1-1	Sell	1	415	-50	3150		23,150
3	12/16	"												20,150
4	12/21	"	L	1	410	1500	1-3	Buy	2	408	+100	(200)		22,950
5	12/29	"	+	1	454	1500								21,450
6	2/2	"	+	2	555	3000		(2200 gain)						19,950
7	2/23	"						(12,300 gain)						16,950
8	3/12	"	S	2	534	3000	1-5,6,7	Sell	4	559	-200	12,900		35,650
9	3/14	"												32,650
10	4/2	"	L	3	535	4500	1-9	Buy	2	504	-100	2900		38,750
11	4/4	"	+	3	576	4500								34,250
12	4/13	"	+	5	680	7500		(6,150 gain)						27,750
13	5/2	"						(37,350 gain)						22,250
14	6/6	"					1-11,12,13	Sell	11	950	-550	185,300		224,050
15														
16								% Gain = 1,020 in 7½ mo.						
17														
18														

36

FIGURE #4 (Cont'd)

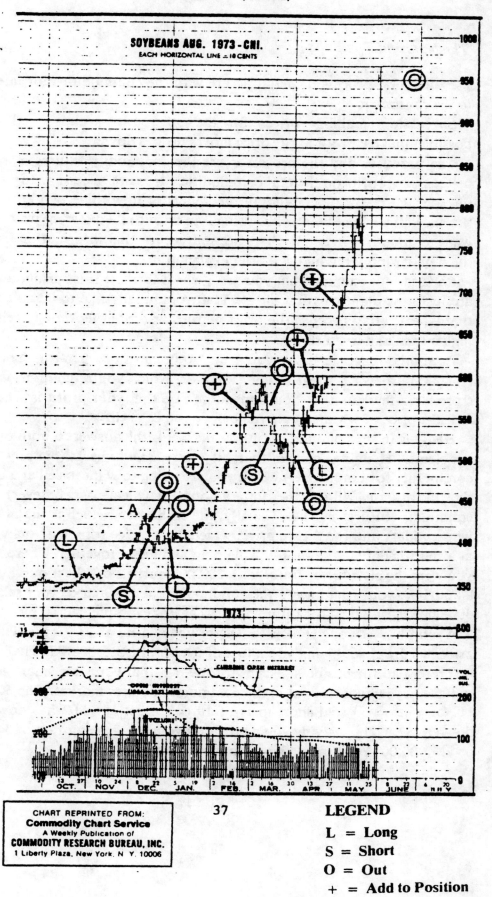

SOYBEANS AUG. 1973 - CHI.
EACH HORIZONTAL LINE = 10 CENTS

37

LEGEND

L = Long
S = Short
O = Out
+ = Add to Position

The Nuts and The Bolts

Processors process or manufacture with the commodities for later sale to the consumers.

Speculators stabilize prices for the other two groups, and, when possible, make a profit as the price moves up and down.

The producer and the processor use the commodity futures market to hedge their profits on the real commodities. It is not necessary for you, as the speculator, to understand all the details of how these two groups use the market, because you will be using it in an entirely different way. If you want to go into it in detail, there are sources for that information listed in the bibliography, but here is a brief explanation.

Let's say for example that you are a wheat farmer. It is spring, and you are just now planting your wheat. You would really like to be able to sell that wheat today because the price of wheat at planting time is generally higher than at harvest time.

In another case, let's say you are a grain elevator operator. You have 500,000 bushels of wheat in your elevator, which you're going to have to store for a few months. You want to be sure that your profit is secure, in case the price of wheat should fall before you can sell.

Hedging in the commodity futures market is the answer to both of these problems. Hedging means that, if you have wheat (or any other commodity for that matter) which you are going to want to sell at a date in the future, you will sell the same amount of wheat (or whatever) in the commodity futures market. Usually, the cash price, which is the price for wheat today, and the future price, which is the price for wheat deliverable at a specific date in the future, will go up and down together. Therefore, if you were the elevator operator with 500,000 bushels of wheat purchased at $4.00/bu., you would go to the commodity futures market and sell short 500,000 bu. of wheat for future delivery at, for example, $4.02/bu.

A month later you get a customer for your wheat at $3.97/bu. The cash price has dropped, giving you a loss of 3¢/bu., or $15,000.00. That would be pretty bad for business, except for the fact that you were smart enough to have hedged your wheat in the commodity futures market. The 500,000 bu. of wheat you sold short in the futures market at $4.02 has now gone down to $3.99/bu., giving you a profit on your futures contract of 3¢/bu., or $15,000.00. Your transaction looks like this:

Wheat bought	@ $4.00/bu.	Futures sold short	@ $4.02/bu.
Wheat sold	@ $3.97/bu.	Futures bought	@ $3.99/bu.
Loss	$ .03/bu.	**Gain**	$ .03/bu.

Of course, this does not give you a net profit, but it does protect you from a loss. As a matter of fact, it rarely happens as neatly as this in real life. In reality, it would generally go one or the other of the following ways:

Wheat bought	@ $4.00/bu.	Futures sold short	@ $4.02/bu.
Wheat sold	@ $4.04/bu.	Futures bought	@ $3.99/bu.
Gain	$ .04/bu.	**Loss**	$ .01/bu.

Net Gain: $.03/bu. or $15,000.

In this case, you made a profit on your actual wheat and took a loss on your futures contract. You might think that it would have been better not to have entered the futures market. Remember, however, that the futures market is your insurance, and it could just as easily have gone this way:

Wheat bought	@ $4.00/bu.	Futures sold short	@ $4.02/bu.
Wheat sold	@ $3.95/bu.	Futures bought	@ $3.94/bu.
Loss	$ .05/bu.	**Gain**	$ .08/bu.

Net gain: $.03/bu. or $15,000.

Your futures insurance pays off and saves you from a loss. Sometimes insurance costs money. Sometimes insurance pays. But having insurance never costs more than not having it.

YOU, THE SPECULATOR, ARE THE MISSING INGREDIENT

The missing ingredient, which is vital to the working of this insurance operation, is the person who is willing to buy when the hedger is selling or sell when the hedger is buying. The person who is willing to assume this risk, in the same way that the life insurance company assumes the risk of your death, is the speculator. You and I, as speculators, are absolutely essential to the smooth functioning of the commodity futures market. Without us to absorb the risk and to provide liquidity, hedging would be impossible and there would be no commodity futures market. Prices in the cash marketplace would be subject to wild fluctuations and the producers and consumers would be at the mercy of these erratic conditions.

HOW THE MARKET WORKS FOR THE SPECULATOR

Stories of tons of wheat being delivered and dumped in your front yard are in the same class of stories as the Boogie Man. These stories do sometimes tend to keep the naive out of the business, but the truth is that as a speculator you don't have to concern yourself with the commodity itself. What you are concerned with is the price, and the movement of the price. You must discipline yourself not to be concerned with what are called the fundamentals. That is, whether the harvest is going well, what the weather is like in Brazil, or whether there is going to be a strike in the copper mines, etc., etc., ad infinitum. I admit that these things do have an effect on the price movement, but the reason you are not concerned with these things is that you will have access to the "Perfect Computer." This amazing "computer" automatically takes all of those things into account, plus millions more that you could not even conceive of, and does it perfectly. You'll learn all about how to use this amazing "computer" later.

You, the speculator, can make money if the price of a commodity goes up, and you can also make money if it goes down. Remember, you do not deal in commodities, but in prices. What you trade are contracts to buy or sell a commodity by a specific date in the future. All commodity contract specifications are standardized by the Exchanges on which they are traded.

Figure #5 gives the specifications of some of the major contracts as of this printing. These specifications seldom change, but before you begin trading, verify them with your broker. I have only given you the contract information that concerns you as a speculator. Contracts are referred to by their delivery month. For example, a contract for wheat deliverable next July is called "July Wheat."

FIGURE 5

BRITISH POUND

Exchange:	International Monetary Market of Chicago Mercantile Exchange (IMM)
Trading Months:	Jan/Mch/Apr/Jun/Jul/Sep/Oct/Dec
Trading Hrs (N.Y.T):	8:30 am to 2:45 pm
Contract Size:	25,000 British pounds
Prices Quoted In:	Dollars/British pound
Min. Price Fluctuation:	5 points
Value Per Point:	$2.50
Daily Trading Limit:	500 points*
Reporting Level:	100 contracts

CATTLE, LIVE

Exchange:	Chicago Mercantile Exchange
Trading Months:	Jan/Feb/Apr/Jun/Aug/Oct/Dec
Trading Hrs (N.Y.T):	10:45 am to 1:45 pm
Contract Size:	40,000 lbs.
Prices Quoted In:	Cents/lb.
Min. Price Fluctuation:	2½ points
Value Per Point:	$4.00
Daily Trading Limit:	150 points
Reporting Level:	100 contracts

COCOA

Exchange:	New York Coffee, Sugar & Cocoa Exchange
Trading Months:	Mch/May/Jul/Sep/Dec
Trading Hrs (N.Y.T):	9:30 am to 3:00 pm
Contract Size:	10 metric tons
Prices Quoted In:	Dollars/metric ton
Min. Price Fluctuation:	$1/ton
Value Per Point:	$10.00
Daily Trading Limit:	88 points*
Reporting Level:	25 contracts

COPPER

Exchange:	Commodity Exchange of New York (COMEX)
Trading Months:	Jan/Mch/May/Jul/Sep/Dec
Trading Hrs (N.Y.T):	9:50 am to 2:00 pm
Contract Size:	25,000 lbs
Prices Quoted In	Cents/lb.
Min. Price Fluctuation:	5 points
Value Per Point:	$2.50
Daily Trading Limit:	500 points*
Reporting Level:	200 contracts

CORN

Exchange:	Chicago Board of Trade
Trading Months:	Mch/May/Jul/Sep/Dec
Trading Hrs (N.Y.T):	10:30 am to 2:15 pm
Contract Size:	5,000 bushels
Prices Quoted In:	Cents/bushel
Min. Price Fluctuation:	¼ cent
Value Per 1¢ Move:	$50.00 (¼ cent = $12.50)
Daily Trading Limit:	10 cents
Reporting Level:	1,000,000 bushels

COTTON NO.2

Exchange:	New York Cotton Exchange
Trading Months:	Mch/May/Jul/Oct/Dec
Trading Hrs (N.Y.T):	10:30 am to 3:00 pm
Contract Size:	50,000 lbs.
Prices Quoted In:	Cents/lb.
Min.Price Fluctuation:	1 point
Value Per Point:	$5.00
Daily Trading Limit:	200 points*
Reporting Level:	50 contracts

DEUTSCHEMARK

Exchange:	International Monetary Market of Chicago Mercantile Exchange (IMM)
Trading Months:	Jan/Mch/Apr/Jun/Jul/Sep/Oct/Dec (plus spot month)
Trading Hrs (N.Y.T):	8:30 am to 2:20 pm
Contract Size:	125,000 Deutschemarks
Prices Quoted In:	Dollars/Deutschemark
Min. Price Fluctuation:	1 point
Value Per Point:	$1.25
Daily Trading Limit:	100 points*
Reporting Level:	100 contracts

GNMA (CDR) MORTGAGE INTEREST RATE FUTURES

Exchange:	Chicago Board of Trade
Trading Months:	Mch/Jun/Sep/Dec
Trading Hrs (N.Y.T):	9:00 am to 3:00 pm
Contract Size:	$100,000
Prices Quoted In:	% of par
Min. Price Fluctuation:	1/32 of 1 point
Value Per Point:	$31.25
Daily Trading Limit:	64/32
Reporting Level:	100 contracts

GOLD

Exchange:	International Monetary Market of Chicago Mercantile Exchange (IMM)
Trading Months:	All months
Trading Hrs (N.Y.T):	9:05 am to 3:00 pm
Contract Size:	100 Troy ounces
Prices Quoted In:	Dollars/Troy ounce
Min. Price Fluctuation:	10 points
Value Per Point:	$1.00
Daily Trading Limit:	$25.00
Reporting Level:	200 contracts

HOGS, LIVE

Exchange:	Chicago Mercantile Exchange
Trading Months:	Feb/Apr/Jun/Jul/Aug/Oct/Dec
Trading Hrs (N.Y.T):	10:10 am to 2:00 pm
Contract Size:	30,000 lbs.
Prices Quoted In:	Cents/lb.
Min. Price Fluctuation:	2½ points
Value Per Point:	$3.00
Daily Trading Limit:	150 points
Reporting Level:	100 contracts

* Trading limit may change under certain circumstances.

41

FIGURE 5 (Cont'd)

JAPANESE YEN

Exchange:	International Monetary Market of Chicago Mercantile Exchange (IMM)
Trading Months:	Jan/Mch/Apr/Jun/Jul/Sep/Oct/Dec (plus spot month)
Trading Hrs (N.Y.T):	8:30 am to 2:22 pm
Contract Size:	12,500,000 Japanese Yen
Prices Quoted In:	Dollars/Japanese Yen
Min. Price Fluctuation:	1 point
Value Per Point:	$1.25
Daily Trading Limit:	100 points*
Reporting Level:	100 contracts

SILVER (NEW)

Exchange:	Chicago Board of Trade
Trading Months:	Feb/Apr/Jun/Aug/Oct/Dec (plus first three months)
Trading Hrs (N.Y.T):	9:05 am to 2:45 pm
Contract Size:	1,000 Troy ounces
Prices Quoted In:	Cents/Troy ounce
Min. Price Fluctuation:	10 points = 1/10 cent/ounce
Value Per Point:	10 Cents
Daily Trading Limit:	60 Cents/ounce ($600/contract)
Reporting Level:	250 contracts

SOYBEAN MEAL

Exchange:	Chicago Board of Trade
Trading Months:	Jan/Mch/May/Jul/Aug/Sep/Oct/Dec
Trading Hrs (N.Y.T):	10:30 am to 2:15 pm
Contract Size:	100 Short tons
Prices Quoted In:	Dollars/short ton
Min. Price Fluctuation:	10 points
Value Per Point:	$1.00
Daily Trading Limit:	1,000 points
Reporting Level:	200 contracts

SOYBEAN OIL

Exchange:	Chicago Board of Trade
Trading Months:	Jan/Mch/May/Jul/Aug/Sep/Oct/Dec
Trading Hrs (N.Y.T):	10:30 am to 2:15 pm
Contract Size:	60,000 lbs.
Price Quoted In:	Cents/lb.
Min. Price Fluctuation:	1 point
Value Per Point:	$6.00
Daily Trading Limit:	100 points
Reporting Level:	200 contracts

SOYBEANS

Exchange:	Chicago Board of Trade
Trading Months:	Jan/Mch/May/Jul/Aug/Sep/Nov
Trading Hrs (N.Y.T):	10:30 am to 2:15 pm
Contract Size:	5,000 bushels
Prices Quoted In:	Cents/bushel
Min. Price Fluctuation:	¼ cent
Value Per 1¢ Move:	$10.00 (1/8 cent = $1.25)
Daily Trading Limit:	30 cents
Reporting Level:	1,000,000 bushels

SUGAR No. 11 (World)

Exchange:	New York Coffee, Sugar & Cocoa Exchange
Trading Months:	Jan/Mch/May/Jul/Sep/Oct
Trading Hrs (N.Y.T):	10:00 am to 1:43 pm (closing call 1:45)
Contract Size:	112,000 lbs (50 long tons)
Prices Quoted In:	Cents/lb.
Min. Price Fluctuation:	1 point
Value Per Point:	$11.20
Daily Trading Limit:	50 points
Reporting Level:	100 contracts

SWISS FRANC

Exchange:	International Monetary Exchange (IMM) of Chicago Mercantile Exchange
Trading months:	Jan/Mch/Apr/May/Jun/Jul/Sep/Oct/Dec (plus spot month)
Trading Hrs (N.Y.T):	8:30 am to 2:16 pm
Contract Size:	125,000 Swiss francs
Prices Quoted In:	Dollars/Swiss francs
Min. Price Fluctuation:	1 point
Value Per Point:	$1.25
Daily Trading Limit:	150 points
Reporting Level:	100 contracts

TREASURY BILLS (90-Day)

Exchange:	International Monetary Exchange (IMM) of Chicago Mercantile Exchange
Trading Months:	Jan/Mch/Apr/Jun/Jul/Sep/Oct/Dec
Trading Hrs (N.Y.T):	9:00 am to 3:00 pm
Contract Size:	$1,000,000
Prices Quoted In:	Index = 100 minus annual discount rate
Min. Price Fluctuation:	1 basis point
Value Per Point:	$25.00
Daily Trading Limit:	50 basis points
Reporting Level:	25 contracts

TREASURY BONDS

Exchange:	Chicago Board of Trade
Trading Months:	Mch/Jun/Sep/Dec
Trading Hrs (N.Y.T):	9:00 am to 3:00 pm
Contract Size:	$100,000
Prices Quoted In:	% of par
Min. Price Fluctuation:	1/32 of 1%
Value Per Point:	$31.25
Daily Trading Limit	64/32
Reporting Level	100 contracts

MARGIN

When you instruct your broker to buy or sell a commodity futures contract, he will require a certain amount of money on deposit with his firm. This is not a down payment on the contract, but a performance bond to insure that you will fulfill the terms of the contract. This deposit is called "margin," and is very low in relation to the cash value of the contract. This low margin is one reason you have so much profit potential when trading commodities. For example, the average margin requirement on the 19 commodities which I recommend trading is about 6.5% of the value of the contracts. By contrast, the margin requirement on stocks is 50%. Is it any wonder that people are flocking to the commodity market? Different brokerage firms will require different amounts of margin, but since they are very competitive, there will generally be little difference.

Now to get on with the speculating. If you think that the price of wheat is going up within the next few days, you would buy one or more contracts of wheat for future delivery. If you think the price of wheat is going down, you would sell short one or more contracts. The next chapter will go into detail on these operations.

THE PERFECT "COMPUTER"

When you learn how to use my trading method you will be using this "computer" to get the data you need to speculate profitably in the commodity futures market. This "computer" can be relied upon with perfect confidence.

One of the fundamental problems in speculating profitably is deciding whether prices are moving up or down. Let me illustrate the difficulty of coming up with this type of accurate information.

There is a wealth of information available today to the speculator. This information is generally divided into two broad categories.

Fundamental data, which is comprised of facts about the commodity itself and general economic conditions, such as weather, planting intentions, inflation, politics, consumption, etc.

Technical data, which consists of the current and past prices of the futures contracts and the pattern of price movement. This data is available on graphs and charts published by various sources.

As I said, there is a flood of information available in both of these areas. In fact, there is so much data available, and so much is necessary for accurate results, that no man-made computer could handle it all.

A classic example of this is what happened to soybean meal a few years ago. The price began to climb for no apparent reason. However, the reason was soon discovered. The Japanese Current, which flows clockwise around the Pacific and along the coast of Peru, had shifted further out to sea. If you had known that the Japanese Current was going to shift, would you have bought soybean meal? Well you should have, because the current is where Peruvian fishermen fish for anchovies and when the current shifted, it took the anchovies too far out to sea for the Peruvian fishermen to go for them, so the supply of anchovy meal was restricted. This short supply of anchovy meal created a huge demand for soybean meal, because both anchovy meal and soybean meal are used as protein supplements in cattle feed.

Now do you see how strange and obscure events can have a profound effect on commodity prices? The vast number of factors, and intricate combinations of factors, which effect the price of commodities is truly astronomical, and no person or ordinary computer could possibly take them all into account, let alone analyze their effect correctly.

SO WHAT IS THIS FABULOUS PERFECT "COMPUTER?"

This perfect "computer" I'm talking about is composed of all the thousands of people who buy and sell in the commodity futures market. The output is the final price, as determined by the bidding on the Exchanges. Our perfect "computer" is the market.

The market automatically takes every conceivable factor into account. Then it takes all those factors and analyzes their effect perfectly. And even if it could be argued theoretically that the market is sometimes wrong, it doesn't matter. Remember that your business is to make money on what the market actually does. Whether it is right or wrong is immaterial. For our purposes, it is always right. It doesn't matter if the weather is bad and the planting is late, or the silver miners are on strike, or the hogs have cholera, or the Russians are buying wheat and the price of cattle *should* be higher. The price of cattle or any other commodity is what the market says it is, and

The Market is Always Right!

This point is so important that I cannot emphasize it enough. Let's say, for example, that you are trading Live Cattle Futures. When you are trading cattle, it is tempting to wonder about how many calves are being born, about the cost of cattle feed, about how severe the winter will be, etc., etc. ad nauseum. But you *must* ignore these fundamentals. Why? Because *you are not trading cattle, you are speculating on the changing price of cattle futures.*

If you try to interpret fundamentals, you may very easily misinterpret them. But the market *never ever* misinterprets the many fundamental factors involved in arriving at a price.

The Market Is Always Right!

I will show you how to use this market data from the "computer" in Chapter Five.

HOW TO PROFIT IF THE PRICE GOES DOWN

There is another concept that must be made clear. If you are an experienced commodity trader you can skip this, but if you're new to commodity speculation, please read this carefully.

It's not hard to understand how profits are made when the price for a commodity is rising, but how about when the price is falling? The fact is, that it is just as easy to profit by price declines as by price advances. This is how it works.

Let's say that the method signals that the price is going to go down. You instruct your broker to *sell* the commodity at today's price and then, when it has finished declining, you instruct him to *buy* it, thus closing out the transaction. The reason you can sell the commodity before you own it is that you are not trading the actual commodity. Remember, you are trading contracts, which are agreements to *sell* by a specific date in the future, at

45

today's price. When the time comes that you want out, since you do not have the real commodity to deliver as you have contracted, you go back into the futures market and *buy* a contract, which is then delivered to fulfill your obligation. This matching of contracts is done by the Exchanges. Thus, you have sold high and *then* bought low for a profit.

In contrast to the stock market, where the rules make it difficult to sell short like this, there are no special rules about short trading in commodities. It is as easy to sell or go short as it is to buy or go long. And as you speculate in the market, you will be short as often as you will be long. It is, therefore, important to be comfortable with the concept.

I think this is all you'll need to know for now about how the market works. However, before we get into the mechanics of the system, I think you need to understand the four laws of profit.

Chapter Four

The Four Laws Of Profit

These laws, or principles, are laws of nature like gravity or electricity, and when properly and consistently applied will guarantee prosperity to any enterprise. These four laws are:

1. The Law of Averages
2. The Law of Leverage
3. The Law of Compounding
4. The Law of Tithing

1. THE LAW OF AVERAGES

The Law of Averages says that the number of times a certain thing will happen is in direct proportion to the number of times it could happen, given a large number of opportunities. The most obvious example is the tossing of a coin. The Law of Averages says that since only two things can happen, each of them will happen half of the time, given a sufficient number of opportunities. As I wrote this, I stopped and tossed an Eisenhower dollar 180 times. Heads came up 87 times, or 48.3% of the time. Tails came up 93 times, or 51.6% of the time. Does this disprove the law of averages? Not in the least. It tells me that I haven't tossed the coin enough times. So, I tossed it another 180 times. This time I came closer to the result predicted by the Law of Averages. Out of the total of 360 tosses, heads came up 179 times, or 49.72%, and tails came up 181 times or 50.27%. The actual record of tosses is shown in Figure #6. As you can see, where there are only two possible outcomes, it doesn't take many chances for the Law of Averages to give us the correct number for each possible occurrence.

Let's take a more complex example. Take a die. It has six sides. How often will the number 6 come up when you toss the die? It can only happen one time out of six. So the Law of Averages says that if you toss the die long enough, 6 will come up on the average of one time out of six, or 16.666667% of the time. You may have streaks with or without the normal number of sixes, but it will eventually even out. The Law of Averages is a law of nature, just like gravity, and it cannot be violated.

If you understand the Law of Averages and apply it to your life, you will eliminate chance and "luck" and your success will be assured. In 1948, Earl Prevette wrote an excellent little book entitled; "How To Turn Your Ability Into Cash." He discussed the Law of Averages, and on page 209 gave this excellent illustration from his own experience selling life insurance.

"Not many years ago, I made 1800 calls over the telephone. I did not get a bite. Was I dismayed? Was I frustrated? Was I discouraged? Not in the least. I was exposing an idea in the form of a sales plan portraying the benefits of life insurance. I was putting into operation the Law of Averages. I knew that this Law could not fail. Operating on this principle, there was no occasion for doubt. I knew that results were certain. What happened? Within a few days, I struck the jackpot. It rained business. Did the Law of Averages pay off? In less than one month I received more than $2.00 for every telephone call I made. (In 1948, $2.00 was not the

FIGURE #6

H	T	H	T	H	T	H	T	H	T	H	T	H	T	H	T	H	T	H	T	H	T	H	T

FIGURE #7

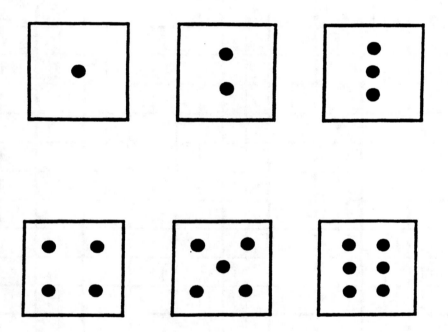

insignificant figure that it is today). In addition, I received a bonus of at least that much more."

Let's take an up-to-date illustration, and apply the Law of Averages to the commodity market. In six years of applying my system to the market, there have been 922 trades, producing an average profit of $525.00 per trade per thousand dollars invested. Of those 922 trades, 424 (or 46%) showed losses. This illustrates the need to have faith in the Law of Averages. Faith in this Law will give you the perseverance you need to accept those losses, knowing that time and the Law of Averages is on your side, working to insure your success.

2. THE LAW OF LEVERAGE

The Law of Leverage, as a principle of physics, is familiar to everyone. However, I'm afraid not enough people understand how this Law works in financial affairs. A lever is a devise by which a little effort on your part can move a large, sometimes otherwise immovable object. If you are a home-owner you are using leverage, probably without thinking about it. In financial affairs the lever is other people's money, sometimes called OPM for short. You are enjoying the benefits of home ownership because someone else was willing to loan you the money to buy that home. Thus, for example, your down payment of $10,000, plus the leverage of $90,000 of OPM, gives you control of the $100,000 home.

In commodity trading, margin gives you leverage. The margin requirement in commodities averages about 6.5% of the value of the commodities you are controlling. For example, a Pork Bellies contract is for 38,000 pounds of pork bellies. Let's say that the price is 70¢ per pound. The value of the whole contract is, therefore, 38,000 x $.70 or $26,600.00. The margin is $2000 per contract, or 7.5%. And you don't pay interest on the balance, as you do on your mortgage or in the stock market. That is a lot of leverage, and is one of the major factors that makes commodity trading so attractive to aggressive investors.

3. THE LAW OF COMPOUNDING

The Law of Compounding means the increasing of your basic investment capital by the addition and reinvestment of the profits. Everyone knows about compound interest on a savings account, but the return is so small that it really doesn't give most of us an idea of the power of compounding. For example, if you had a 10% return compounded monthly, it would look like th'

Compounded			Not Compounded		
Investment	Gain	Total	Investment	Gain	Total
$100	$10	$110	$100	$10	$110
$110	$11	$121	$100	$10	$120
$121	$12	$133	$100	$10	$130
$133	$13	$146	$100	$10	$140
$146	$15	$161	$100	$10	$150
$161	$16	$177	$100	$10	$160
$177	$18	$195	$100	$10	$170
$195	$20	$215	$100	$10	$180
$215	$22	$237	$100	$10	$190
$237	$24	$261	$100	$10	$200
$261	$26	$287	$100	$10	$210

The difference is quite obvious. By compounding, over a twelve month period, you have earned **$96** more than you would have by not compounding. The real power of compounding comes to light as you continue. The longer you continue the process, the faster it grows. For example, if these two programs were continued, the results would be as follows:

Year	Compounding	Not Compounding
1	$ 316	$220
2	$ 993	$340
3	$ 3,132	$460
4	$ 9,834	$580
5	$30,864	$700
6	$96,867	$820

The difference is indeed startling, is it not? Now let's apply this principle to a typical commodity account using my trading system. In this example, you have invested $50,000 in the beginning, and realize a very conservative 100% gain each year. Also, in order to make it more realistic, because you want to use some of your new wealth to improve your lifestyle, let's

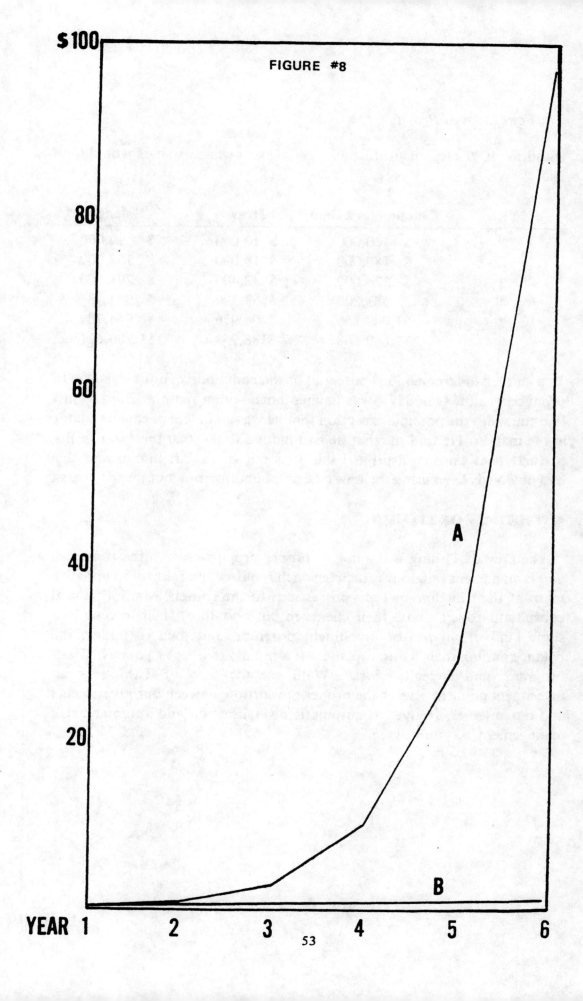

FIGURE #8

withdraw 10% of your profit each year. This is what six years would look like.

Year	Compounded Gain	Draw	Balance
1	$ 100,000	$ 10,000	$ 90,000
2	$ 180,000	$ 18,000	$ 162,000
3	$ 324,000	$ 32,400	$ 291,600
4	$ 583,200	$ 58,320	$ 944,784
5	$1,049,760	$104,976	$ 944,784
6	$1,889,568	$188,957	$1,700,611

You can see the tremendous potential of the commodity futures market to produce wealth. One day I was having lunch with a man in Chicago just like you, with the possible exception that he was an independent speculator in the market. He told me that he had made $50,000,000 that year in the market. That's not a misprint. I said fifty million dollars in one year! He had obviously been using the Law of Compounding for a number of years.

4. THE LAW OF TITHING

The Law of Tithing is the law of proper proportion. A tithe is a tenth and is an ancient religious principle which required the faithful to donate a tenth of their income or their possessions to the church. Many financial consultants today advise their clients to put a tenth of their income into some kind of savings or investment program, and then to budget the balance among their living expenses. It amounts to a "pay yourself first" program, and it really works. We'll use the Law of Tithing as an investment guide to give us the proper proportion between our investments and our reserves. It gives us automatic diversification and automatic risk management, as you will see.

Chapter Five

The Ups And The Downs
And How To Tell The Difference

Everyone knows how nice it is to be long when the market is rising and short when the market is falling, so let's get down to business. What I'm going to give you here is a trading system which requires no market analysis, but which will tell you which way the market is going to go each and every day—with 70% to 80% accuracy!

As you know, the market will make a large number of small movements for every one big move it makes. Unfortunately, no one, and I mean *no one*, can tell in advance when one of those small moves is going to be the beginning of the big move. Therefore, you have to follow each move, and get out quickly if it fails. When a small move fails to become a big one, it is not a failure on your part or a failure of the trading system. It isn't even a failure of the market. It's just a short move. But we can't make much money on a short move, so we get out quickly and accept our small profit or loss. Remember, the market is always right, and the Law of Averages is on your side. Don't fight it—use it.

HOW MUCH MONEY DOES IT TAKE TO START?

The minimum amount of capital needed to start trading commodity futures is determined in the following manner. First, add up the margin requirements for the eighteen commodities that I recommend. Second, multiply the total by five.

For example, at this writing, the margin requirements for the eighteen commodities were as follows:

Corn	$ 500	Pork Bellies	$1200	Deutschemark	$1500
Soybeans	$1500	Cocoa	$1500	British Pound	$1500
Soy Meal	$1000	Sugar	$2000	Japanese Yen	$1500
Soy Oil	$ 600	Copper	$ 700	Swiss Franc	$2000
Cattle	$ 900	Gold	$2000	T-Bills	$ 900
Hogs	$ 800	Silver	$1000	S & P 500	$6000

The total margin is $27,100. Multiplied by 5, it equals $135,500. If $135,500 is a little beyond your budget, choose whichever portfolio listed below fits your starting capital. As your capital increases, add one commodity at a time to your portfolio in the order they are listed here.

COMMODITY	MARGIN REQUIRED	CAPITAL REQUIRED
1. Pork Bellies	$1200	$ 6,000
2. Soybeans	$1500	$ 13,500
3. German Mark	$1500	$ 21,000
4. Copper	$ 700	$ 24,500
5. Gold (CMX)	$2000	$ 34,500
6. Sugar (world)	$2000	$ 44,500
7. Corn	$ 500	$ 47,000
8. Soybean Oil	$ 600	$ 50,000
9. Treasury Bills	$ 900	$ 54,500
10. Live Cattle	$ 900	$ 59,000
11. Soybean Meal	$1000	$ 64,000
12. Silver (CMX)	$1000	$ 69,000
13. Live Hogs	$ 800	$ 73,000
14. Swiss Franc	$2000	$ 83,000
15. Japanese Yen	$1500	$ 90,500
16. Cocoa	$1500	$ 98,000
17. British Pound	$1500	$105,500
18. S & P 500	$6000	$135,500

For example, if you have $50,000 to invest, choose number 8 which contains Pork Bellies, Soybeans, German Marks, Gold, Copper, Sugar, Corn and Soybean Oil. As your capital increases, add one commodity at a time in the order given.

HOW TO KEEP TRACK OF THE UPS AND THE DOWNS

The best way to keep track of the ups and downs of the price of the various commodities which you are following is with the standard bar chart (see Figure #9). You will have to keep your own charts of the daily price action of the commodities you are trading. There is no need to subscribe to a chart service. What you get from them is last week's charts, and that doesn't do you any good at all. You will still have to keep their chart up to date during the current week yourself, so why not just make your own charts to begin with and save the cost of buying theirs? In

57

FIGURE #9

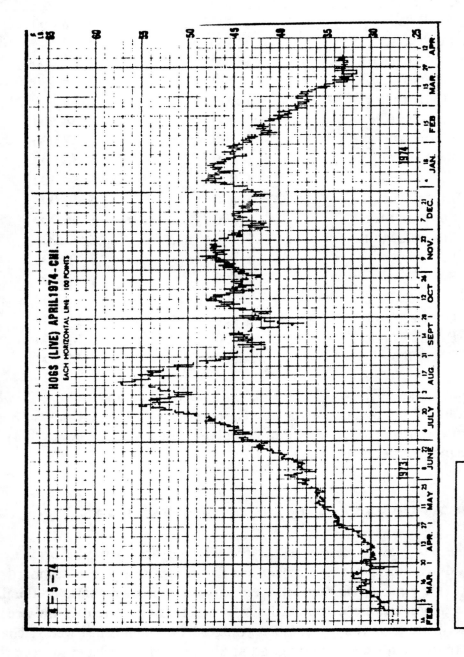

58

addition to that, the chart services give you a lot of information that you don't need or want. Get some graph paper that is "10 lines to the inch" and make your own charts. The Keuffel & Esser Co. makes a commodity chart paper. It's #47 1810 and it will hold a whole year of trading on one sheet. They also make a binder to hold these sheets.

THE KEY TO MY TRADING SYSTEM IS "THE SIGNAL"

It is amazing to me that no one, up to now, has recognized this signal for what it is. The reason is probably because it is so simple. As far as I know, this is the first time this signal has been written about, and the first time it has been integrated into a trading system. This simple little signal will tell you, each day, which way the market will go the following trading day.

Here is how to get the signal. After the market closes each day, plot the high-low range and the settlement price. If today's high is higher than yesterday's high, and the closing price today is above the middle of today's range, it is an indication of upward sentiment in the market. Tomorrow's close will very likely be above today's close. The reverse is also true. If today's low is lower than yesterday's low, and the close is below the middle of today's range, it is an indication of downward sentiment. Tomorrow's close is likely to be lower than today's close. If neither occurs, the signal is neutral, indicating indecisiveness.

A These are all **up** signals.

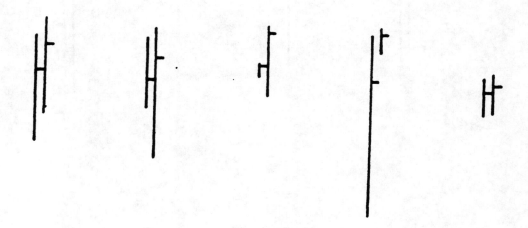

59

B These are all **down** signals.

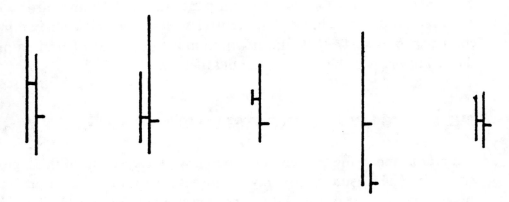

C These are all **neutral** signals.

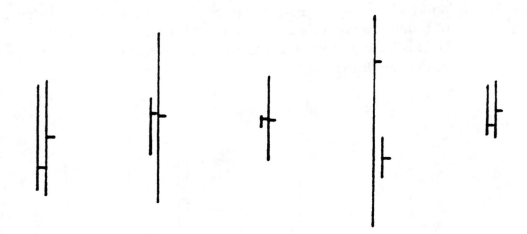

It is very simple to spot the mood of the market this way, and it is amazingly reliable. Its reliability will vary from commodity to commodity and from time to time, but overall it will be correct 55 to 75 percent of the time.

If you get an **up** signal, it means most traders are bullish. You don't care why they're bullish. You don't care where they got their information or what their decision is based upon.

The fact is, that since traders make the price by open auction, the price will go the way they say it will go.

There is one qualification on the mid-range or indecisive closing. Let's say you are in a trend, meaning you have been in a position for a number of days, and your profits are good. If it looks today like the market is going to close at or near the mid-range, wait as long as you can before making a decision, and then if the close is going to be at the mid-range or in the same direction you have been going, stay with it. What you are balancing is the cost of a brokerage commission to get out today and back in tomorrow, against the loss you might experience if the market is changing direction. If the market is so indecisive today, it is not likely to go very far against you tomorrow. And it may just keep on in the same direction. However, if you get out, the loss of the brokerage commission is a sure thing. Therefore, the odds favor staying in the position.

HOW TO USE "THE SIGNAL" TO BUY AND SELL

In this explanation we will assume an upward trend, but the same rules apply for a downward trend. When the high is higher than yesterday's high and the market closes above the midpoint of the day's range, it is an indication of bullish sentiment. The market wants to go up. When this happens three days in a row, it is a signal to buy. See Figure #10. The third day is the day on which you must take action. On the third day, watch the market closely. Or have your broker do so. When it becomes clear that the close is going to be above the midpoint, take a long position.

FIGURE #10

A. These are all signals to sell **short**.

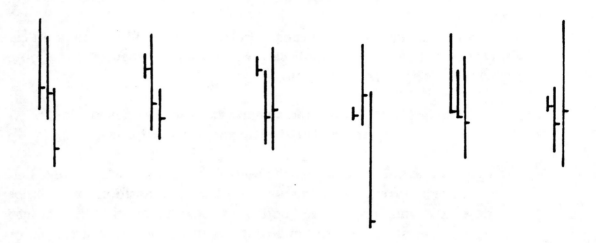

B. These are all signals to buy **long**.

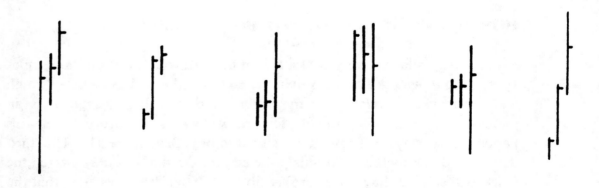

There is one variation on the three day rule. If there is a gap before the first or second day, the gap counts as a day and the second day becomes the day on which you take action. See Figure #11.

Between 70 and 80 percent of the time, this three day signal will be followed by a significant move in the direction indicated. Get some charts and see for yourself how often this signal occurs at or near the beginning of large moves.

Now that you see how simple this rule is, you should test it on paper without investing any money for awhile, in order to convince yourself of how well it works.

USING THE SIGNAL TO GET OUT

Getting out of a position at the right time is generally the most difficult aspect of trading the market, but the signal makes it automatic. It works like this.

Stay in your position until you get a signal in the opposite direction, then close out your position and take a position in the opposite direction.

NEVER MEET A MARGIN CALL

There is one other rule about getting out which has nothing to do with the signal. That is, you should *never meet a margin call.* If you get a margin call, just instruct your broker to close out your position. In fact, the best thing is to instruct your broker, in advance, that when any of your positions require additional margin, that he is to just close them out.

FIGURE #11

A. These are all signals to buy **long**.

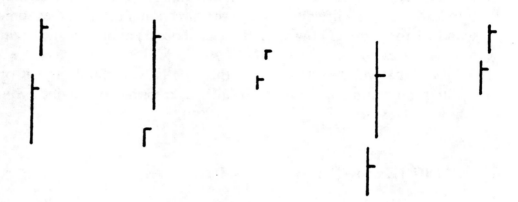

B. These are all signals to sell **short**.

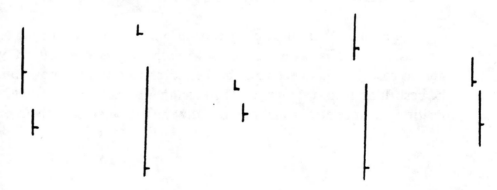

Chapter Six

The Complete Trading Plan

As powerful as the signal is, it does not, of course, in and of itself, constitute a complete trading system. It should be integrated into a complete trading system which consists of the following additional rules.

RULE #1   DIVERSIFICATION

Each commodity will act differently from the others. While one will be moving up or down vigorously, another may be just going sideways. It would be nice if you could always just trade those commodities which were moving up or down, but that is not always possible. Remember that the Law of Averages works best if there are a large number of events. Therefore, if you trade 2, 3 or more different commodities, you will have a better chance of catching the best moves. I recommend that you follow and trade as many of the nineteen commodities as your capital will allow. These are currently the most actively traded commodities, and they have high volatility or movement with large volume. This is vital to your trading because if you are ready to sell and there is no one to buy, or ready to buy and there is no one willing to sell to you, it could cost you a lot of money. So you are going to trade as many of these active commodities as your capital will allow, in accordance with the Law of the Tithe.

RULE #2   CONSISTENCY

This trading system is tremendously powerful at producing profits *if it is followed without deviation!* You must try this technique on paper until you have complete faith in it. I cannot emphasize enough that once you invest money in the market, you must not deviate from the rules. I can guarantee you that the minute you think that you are smarter than the market, you will lose your *shirt!!!* As soon as you decide that a certain commodity is just going sideways and stop trading it, just at that moment it will begin that big move you've been waiting for. Trade with the signals. If a given signal is for a short move or is incorrect, a new signal or a margin call will get you out with a small loss. If it is that big move you've been waiting for, the signal will keep you in it until the move is over and then a new signal will get you out with a big profit. The Law of Averages is on your side, and the market is always right!

Don't listen to news!
Don't listen to your broker!
Don't listen to tips!
Don't subscribe to an advisory service!
Don't let your broker send you his firm's newsletter!
Don't watch the market during the trading day!

Any one or any combination of these things will give you incomplete data, which will very likely cause you to do something stupid, and will cost you money.

Just like "The Shadow,"
the market knows what lurks in the hearts of traders,
and the signal will tell you what the market knows.

RULE #3   TITHE YOUR EQUITY

This means that when entering a new position or when adding to an existing position, you should go long or short as many contracts as you can with ten percent (10%) of your available equity. Available equity is the cash in your account which is not committed as margin, plus all unrealized profits on positions which you hold. Because of his computerized accounting methods, your broker will know your equity position every day. If he does not, get a broker who does.

Ten percent is very easy to calculate, and to find the number of contracts to buy or sell short, you merely divide the margin required per contract into the ten percent figure.

$$\frac{\text{Available Equity X .1}}{\text{Margin}} = \text{Number of Contracts}$$

For example:

$$\frac{\$27,586 \text{ X } .1}{\$1,600} = 1.724 \text{ or 2 contracts}$$
(Round off to the nearest unit).

$$\frac{\$59,984 \text{ X } .1}{\$1,600} = 3.749 \text{ or 4 contracts}$$

$$\frac{\$98,084 \text{ X } .1}{\$1,600} = 6.130 \text{ or 6 contracts}$$

If you put the Law of Tithing to work for you, it will *automatically* do the following five things for you which are absolutely essential, but which you might not do if you didn't have a rule to follow.

(1) It will automatically diversify your funds into a sufficient number of different commodities so that a loss in one or two will not put you out of business.

(2) It will automatically keep you from being too heavily committed to any one position. It is a common, and I stress common, cause of failure in this business to chase after a good move with more and more money until it all comes apart in a quick reversal and everything is lost. **Follow the rules.**

(3) It will automatically keep your risk to a minimum. Keeping risk manageable is one of the most important aspects of any business. It is especially important in this business, because risk is what it's all about. Instead of risking everything to make a possible $100,000 on one move, risk 10% of your equity and make $20,000 five times during the year. You will still make $100,000, but with only 1/10th of the risk. **Follow the rules.**

(4) It will automatically increase the number of contracts you trade and the size of your profits as your capital increases. It is this aspect of the rules that will build your fortune, even though it does it carefully and conservatively. This seemingly simple Law of the Tithe, when consistently applied, is the most powerful money management tool imaginable. Figure #12 illustrates the power of this tool.

Line A illustrates your equity when investing by the Law of the Tithe.

Line B illustrates your equity when investing the same amount on each signal.

(5) It will automatically keep you from ever committing all of your funds to the market. Even if you were in all eighteen positions at the same time, you would have a reserve. It works like this.

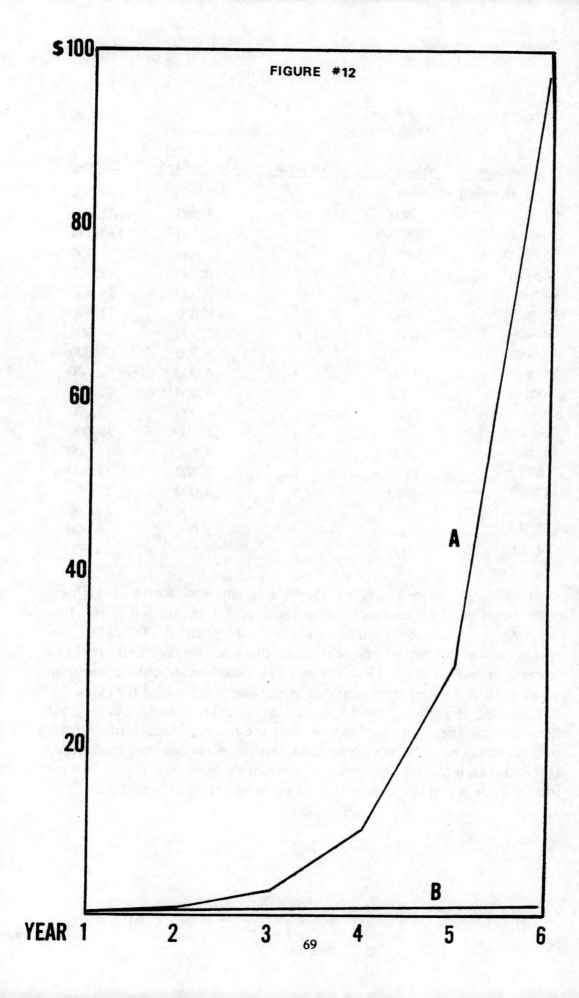

FIGURE #12

Contract	Margin	# of Cont.	Margin Committed	Balance
Opening Balance				135,500
Corn	500	27	13,500	122,000
Soybeans	1500	8	12,000	110,000
Soy Meal	1000	11	11,000	99,000
Soy Oil	600	17	10,200	88,800
Cattle	900	10	9,000	79,800
Hogs	800	10	8,000	71,800
Bellies	1200	6	7,200	64,600
Cocoa	1500	4	6,000	58,600
Sugar	2000	3	6,000	52,600
Copper	700	8	5,600	47,000
Gold	2000	2	4,000	43,000
Silver	1000	4	4,000	39,000
Pound	1500	3	4,500	34,500
Yen	1500	2	3,000	31,500
Franc	2000	2	4,000	27,500
German Mark	1500	2	3,000	24,500
S & P 500	6000	1	6,000	18,500
T-Bills	2000	1	2,000	16,500

You have only used 87.8% of your funds and you are in all eighteen positions at once. Of course, it will never happen like this in real life. This is merely a mathematical model to illustrate the principle. In reality, you would have gotten out of one or more of these positions or had profits or losses in some of them. Nevertheless, you could never have more than about 88% of your equity committed at any one time. **Follow the rules.**

Following the rules takes the agony of decision making out of your hands. Remember, you don't know what the market is going to do from one day to the next. I don't know either, and neither does your broker. *No individual knows what the market is going to do from day to day.* But the market knows, and you are now tapping that source of information.

RULE #4   PYRAMID YOUR PROFITS

In spite of the bad reputation that pyramiding has gotten, you must pyramid your profits in order to get the most out of your opportunities. There are two traditional ways of pyramiding. One acceptable and the other unacceptable. I feel that my method is better than either one. This is the way that it works.

If you are in a profitable position, and the market gives a new signal in the same direction, add more contracts to your position on the same basis as when you took the original position. That is, with ten percent of your equity (See Rule #3).

Those are the trading rules. You are now ready to test them on paper in order to gain the faith and confidence you will need when your money is on the line. There is only one other thing left to do before you are ready to commit your funds to the market. You must choose a broker.

CHOOSING A BROKER

A good broker is important to the effective working of this system. Therefore, it is very important that you choose him well. He must be willing to accept the fact that you do not want any advice from him or his firm. He must be a trader, and not just an order-taker like most brokers. Find a broker who manages accounts. He is a trader. But remember, he is not going to manage your account. Get a broker who lives and works in Chicago. Chicago is where most of the trading is done. Your broker should be personally acquainted with the floor traders. He can do a better job for you than your local broker, no matter what a local broker may say. Your local broker will tell you that, because of the marvels of modern communication, he is just as close to the trading floor as a man in Chicago. The action is not at your local broker's office. Since you only need to contact your broker by telephone, and since he pays the phone bill, it is better for you to have your broker in Chicago, where the business is conducted.

YOU'RE ON YOUR WAY

You are now on the way to profits in the commodity futures market. I cannot guarantee your success, nor can I guarantee that you will not lose your shirt, because I cannot control how you use my system. Remember that this is a business, not a game. It will take discipline and patience and faith in yourself and in the system for you to succeed. I know that the system can do what I claim it can. If you have the discipline, patience and faith in yourself and the system, you will become independently wealthy.

APPENDICES

Appendix I

Glossary

Bear—a trader who thinks that prices are declining.

Bull—a trader who thinks that prices are rising.

Commission—the fee a broker charges for his services.

Contract—an agreement to buy or sell a specific quantity of a particular commodity by a specified date. Specifications of all contracts are established by the Exchange on which the contract is traded.

Limit Move—the maximum increase or decrease a price may move in relation to the previous day's close.

Long—noun, being a buyer; verb, buying a market position.

Margin—a performance bond deposited with a broker when taking a long or short position in the market.

Margin Call—a demand to increase the amount of margin on deposit to acceptable minimums.

Range—the difference between the highest and the lowest price on a given trading day.

Settlement Price—the official closing price of a specific commodity contract each trading day.

Short—noun, being a seller; verb, selling a market position.

Spot—the price of the commodity for immediate delivery. The spot month is the current month.

Trading Limit—the amount a price may change from the previous day's close.

Appendix II

Bibliography

Gould, Bruce, **Commodity Trading Manual,** Bruce Gould Publications, Seattle, Wash., 1976.

Hieronymus, Thomas A., **Economics of Futures Trading,** Commodity Research Bureau, New York, 1971.

Prevette, Earl, **How to Turn Your Ability Into Cash,** 1948.

Teweles, Richard J., Stone, Herbert L., and Harlow, Charles V., **The Commodity Futures Game, Who Wins? Who Loses? Why?,** McGraw-Hill, New York, 1974.

Williams, Larry, **How I Made $1,000,000 Trading Commodities Last Year,** Windsor Books, Brightwaters, N.Y. 11718, 1973.